Copyright © 2024 Grow Grit Press LLC. All rights reserved. No part of this book may be reproduced in any form without permission in writing from the publisher. Please send bulk order requests to info@ninjalifehacks.tv

Paperback ISBN: 978-1-63731-987-1
Hardcover ISBN: 978-1-63731-989-5
eBook ISBN: 978-1-63731-988-8

Printed and bound in the USA.
NinjaLifeHacks.tv

Ninja Life Hacks®
by Mary Nhin

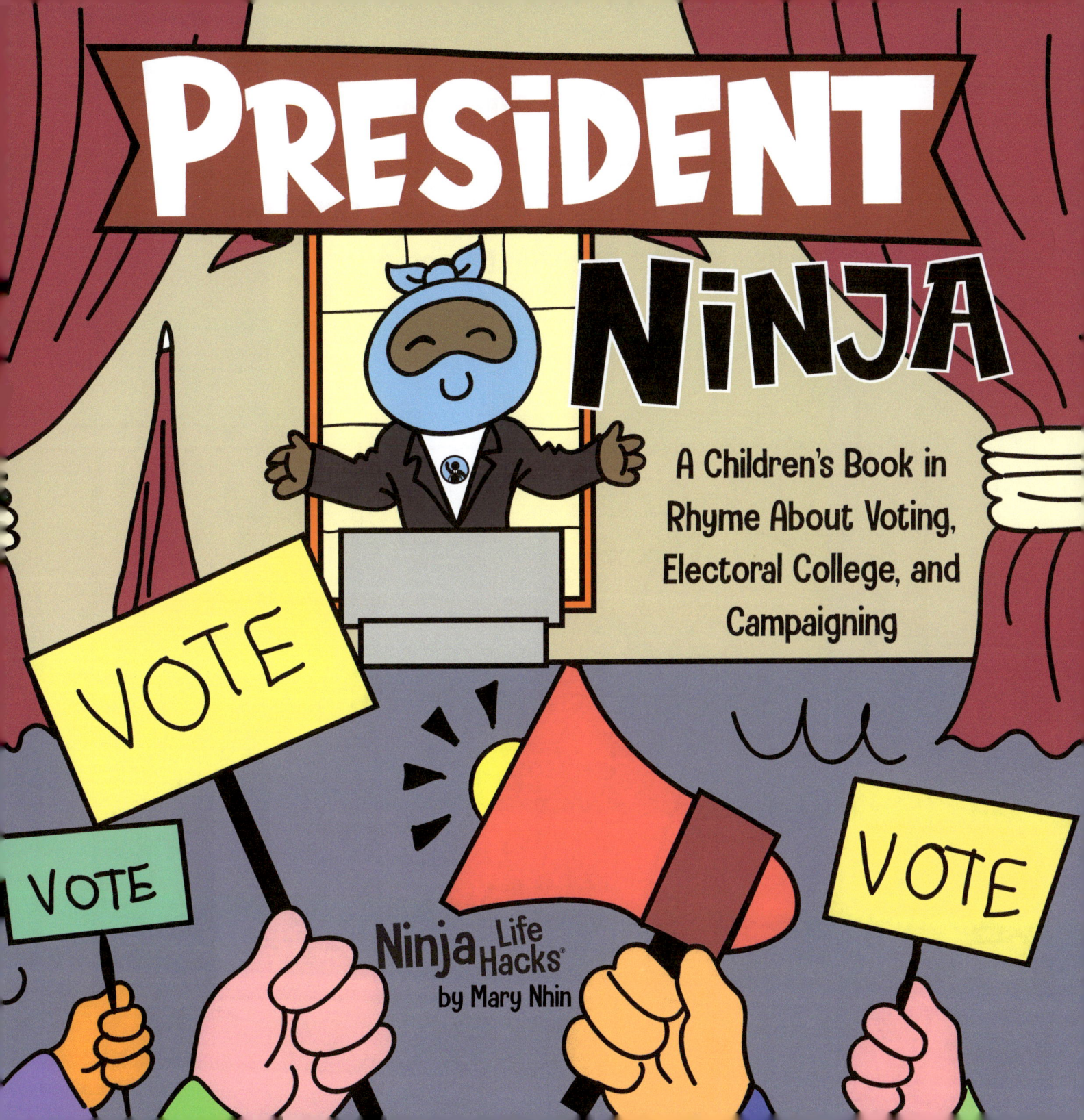

In a school where ninjas learned,
A big election came.
Two kids from different classrooms ran
To earn the president's name.

I made bright signs and catchy logos,
With rhymes to make them fun.
"Better Lunch, Longer Fun—
Ninja Gets It Done!"

I felt a flutter in my heart,
To stand and speak was tough.
But I knew I'd make a change,
My voice was strong enough.

Continue the learning with President Ninja's lesson plans at ninjalifehacks.tv

Create Your Own Campaign Poster

Objective: Make a campaign poster for a school election, just like President Ninja did!

Supplies needed:

✓ Large sheet of paper or poster board

✓ Markers, crayons, or paint

✓ Scissors

✓ Glue

✓ Stickers, glitter, or other decorations

✓ Optional: Photos or drawings of the candidate

Instructions:

1. Choose a candidate or make one up—this could be you, a friend, or even a character like President Ninja!
2. On the large sheet of paper, write the name of your candidate in big, bold letters at the top.
3. Use markers or paint to add a slogan, like "Better Lunch, Longer Fun—Ninja Gets It Done!"
4. Draw or glue on pictures that represent the candidate's goals—like a soccer ball for more recess, or a lunch tray for better meals.
5. Decorate the poster with stickers, glitter, or anything else that makes it stand out.
6. Display your poster in your room or classroom to inspire others!

"Better Lunch, Longer FUN
↪ NINJA Gets It DONe!"

Build a Mini Voting Booth

Objective: Make a voting booth and ballot box. Then, vote on your favorite snack, food, school supply, and/or pet!

Supplies needed:

- ✓ Cardboard box or shoebox
- ✓ Construction paper
- ✓ Scissors
- ✓ Glue or tape
- ✓ Markers or crayons
- ✓ Small slips of paper (for ballots)
- ✓ A small container (for the ballot box)

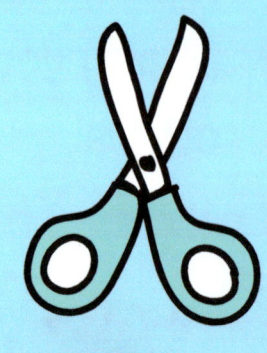

Instructions:

1. Use the cardboard box as the base for your voting booth. Cut an opening on one side where voters can put in their ballots.
2. Cover the box with construction paper, decorating it with words like "Voting Booth" and adding designs like stars or stripes.
3. Use additional pieces of cardboard to create a privacy screen around the opening, where voters can stand behind while voting.
4. Create small ballots by cutting slips of paper. Write the names of the candidates on the ballots.
5. Place a small container or another box near the voting booth to serve as the ballot box.
6. Set up your mini voting booth and have your friends or family vote for their favorite candidate. Afterward, count the ballots and announce the winner!

www.ingramcontent.com/pod-product-compliance
Lightning Source LLC
Chambersburg PA
CBHW041710160426
43209CB00018B/1794